4/14

TEAM SPIRIT®

SMART BOOKS FOR YOUNG FANS

THE EDMONTON OILERS

BY

MARK STEWART

CONTENT CONSULTANT
DENIS GIBBONS
SOCIETY FOR INTERNATIONAL HOCKEY RESEARCH

NORWOOD HOUSE PRESS

CHICAGO, ILLINOIS

Norwood House Press
P.O. Box 316598
Chicago, Illinois 60631

For information regarding Norwood House Press, please visit our website at:
www.norwoodhousepress.com or call 866-565-2900.

All photos courtesy of Associated Press except the following:
O-Pee-Chee Ltd. (6, 15, 45), Edmonton Oilers (7, 33), Hockey Hall of Fame (8, 16, 17, 25, 27, 31, 35, 37, 38),
Tiger Press, Inc. (9), Esso/Imperial Oil Ltd. (10), Topps, Inc. (19, 22, 41, 43 top),
Quarton Group/NHL (26, 42 bottom), Author's Collection (34, 42 top), The Upper Deck Company (40).
Cover Photo: AP Photo/The Canadian Press, Ian Jackson

The memorabilia and artifacts pictured in this book are presented for educational and informational purposes,
and come from the collection of the author.

Editor: Mike Kennedy
Designer: Ron Jaffe
Project Management: Black Book Partners, LLC.
Special thanks to Topps, Inc.

Library of Congress Cataloging-in-Publication Data

Stewart, Mark, 1960 July 7-
    The Edmonton Oilers / by Mark Stewart.
        pages cm. -- (Team spirit)
    Includes bibliographical references and index.
    Summary: "A revised Team Spirit Hockey edition featuring the Edmonton
Oilers that chronicles the history and accomplishments of the team. Includes
access to the Team Spirit website which provides additional information and
photos"-- Provided by publisher.
    ISBN 978-1-59953-620-0 (library edition : alk. paper) -- ISBN
978-1-60357-628-4 (ebook) 1. Edmonton Oilers (Hockey
team)--History--Juvenile literature. I. Title.
    GV848.E36S74 2014
    796.962'6409712334--dc23
                                                            2013030875

239N—012014
Manufactured in the United States of America in Stevens Point, Wisconsin.

COVER PHOTO: The Oilers celebrate a goal in front of their excited hometown fans.

TABLE OF CONTENTS

CHAPTER	PAGE
MEET THE OILERS	4
GLORY DAYS	6
HOME ICE	12
DRESSED FOR SUCCESS	14
WE WON!	16
GO-TO GUYS	20
CALLING THE SHOTS	24
ONE GREAT DAY	26
LEGEND HAS IT	28
IT REALLY HAPPENED	30
TEAM SPIRIT	32
TIMELINE	34
FUN FACTS	36
TALKING HOCKEY	38
GREAT DEBATES	40
FOR THE RECORD	42
PINPOINTS	44
GLOSSARY	46
LINE CHANGE	47
INDEX	48

ABOUT OUR GLOSSARY

In this book, there may be several words that you are reading for the first time. Some are sports words, some are new vocabulary words, and some are familiar words that are used in an unusual way. All of these words are defined on page 46. Throughout the book, sports words appear in **bold type**. Regular vocabulary words appear in ***bold italic type***.

MEET THE OILERS

No large city in Canada is farther north than Edmonton. Not surprisingly, ice hockey is a major part of daily life there. Kids start playing hockey soon after they can walk. They watch the game their entire lives. And they cheer for the Edmonton Oilers.

Other hockey teams played in Edmonton before the Oilers, but they were the first club to win the **Stanley Cup**. In fact, for a 10-year period in the 1980s, they were the most exciting team anyone had ever seen. Indeed, the wide-open style that brings fans to their feet today really began when the Oilers joined the **National Hockey League (NHL)**.

This book tells the story of the Oilers. More so than any club in recent memory, they created a *blueprint* for building a championship team. They showed that talent only takes you so far—smart, unselfish play gets you the rest of the way. Many clubs have copied the Oilers, but no one has done it better.

Sam Gagner joins Nail Yakupov and Taylor Hall to celebrate a goal during a 2012–13 game.

GLORY DAYS

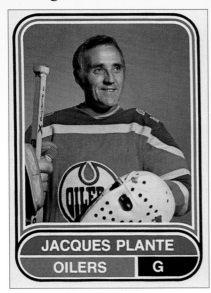

JACQUES PLANTE
OILERS | **G**

n the early 1970s, North America caught a case of "hockey fever." The NHL grew from six teams to 18 in a seven-year period. In 1972, the **World Hockey Association (WHA)** began with 12 teams, including the Alberta Oilers, who played in Edmonton. The best player to sign with the Oilers was defenseman Al Hamilton of the Buffalo Sabres. Jim Harrison, a center from the Toronto Maple Leafs, was the Oilers' leading scorer their first season.

In their second year, the Oilers officially made Edmonton their home. Over the next few seasons, the team added more talent, including Barry Long, Blair McDonald, and Bill Flett. Goalie Jacques Plante joined the team in 1974 for his final season at the age of 46! Dave Dryden replaced Plante the following year and was voted the league's **Most Valuable Player (MVP)** in 1978–79.

That season, the Oilers made it to the AVCO Cup Finals, the WHA's championship series. Dave Langevin and Paul Shmyr led the defense, while a talented teenager named Wayne Gretzky powered the offense. Gretzky led the team in scoring with 104 points (goals plus **assists**) in 72 games. He also scored 20 points in 13 games in the **playoffs**, but the Oilers fell to the Winnipeg Jets in the finals.

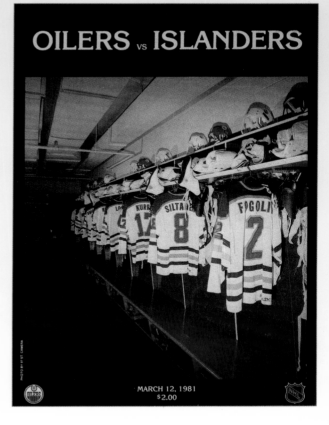

OILERS vs ISLANDERS

MARCH 12, 1981
$2.00

Over the following summer, the NHL invited four WHA clubs to join the league, including the Oilers. Coach Glen Sather built an excellent team around Gretzky, who quickly showed that he was head and shoulders above anyone else in the game. In 1980–81, "The Great One" scored 55 goals and set an NHL record with 109 assists. In 1981–82, he shattered the NHL mark of 76 goals when he netted 92. The following season, Gretzky led the Oilers to the **Stanley Cup Finals** for the first time in team history. But the New York Islanders were too much to handle, and Edmonton lost in four games.

LEFT: Jacques Plante finished his record-breaking career with the Oilers.
ABOVE: Edmonton fans bought this program during the team's first trip to the Stanley Cup Finals.

The Oilers played a fast, wide-open brand of hockey that caught most NHL teams by surprise. Edmonton could turn a good save or defensive play in its own end into a scoring opportunity the other way in the blink of an eye. Gretzky was the team's leader, but he had plenty of help from other talented young stars. Forwards Mark Messier, Jari Kurri, and Glenn Anderson were dangerous scorers. Defensemen Kevin Lowe and Paul Coffey combined with goalie Grant Fuhr to keep opponents off the scoreboard. Many of these players would one day join Gretzky in the **Hall of Fame**.

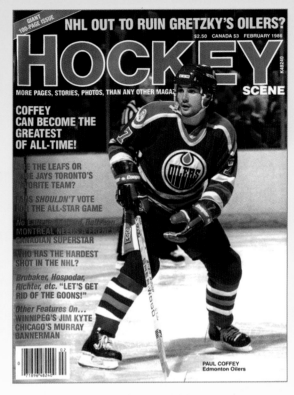

Edmonton turned to Gretzky as the new team captain in 1983–84. This gave the club the extra charge it needed. The Oilers set a league record for goals and returned to the Stanley Cup Finals. The Oilers won their first Stanley Cup that spring, and Messier was awarded the Conn Smythe Trophy as **postseason** MVP. They won another championship in 1984–85, as Gretzky set a playoff record with 47 points and Coffey broke several scoring marks for defensemen. Edmonton won the championship again in 1986–87.

LEFT: Wayne Gretzky earned the nickname "The Great One" while playing for the Oilers.   **ABOVE**: As a young player, Paul Coffey was already being compared to the all-time greats.

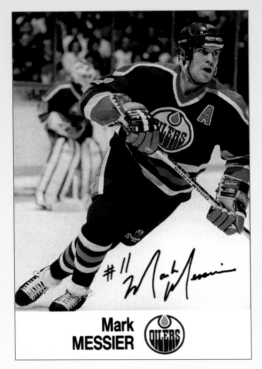

Mark
MESSIER

The team captured its fourth NHL crown in 1987–88.

After winning four Stanley Cups in five years, Gretzky decided to move on. The Oilers *obliged* and traded him to the Los Angeles Kings for young stars Jimmy Carson and Martin Gelinas, as well as several high **draft choices**. Edmonton fans were outraged, as was the rest of Canada. One politician asked the Canadian government to stop the trade!

The loss of Gretzky put the pressure on Messier. In 1989–90, he led the rebuilt Oilers to their fifth Stanley Cup. Their playoff run included several dramatic comebacks and—best of all—a four-game sweep of Gretzky and the Kings. The Oilers played almost the entire year without Fuhr in goal. His replacement, Bill Ranford, was sensational against the Boston Bruins in the championship series.

The Oilers fell on hard times in the 1990s. Among the top players who wore the Edmonton uniform during this time were Todd Marchant, Jason Arnott, Doug Weight, Petr Klima, Ryan Smyth, and Curtis Joseph. Things began to look up in 2005–06. The Oilers had added stars such as Michael Peca, Chris Pronger,

Sergei Samsonov, and Dwayne Roloson. They joined a core of young players, including Smyth, Shawn Horcoff, Raffi Torres, Jarret Stoll, and Ales Hemsky. Edmonton made the playoffs and **upset** the Detroit Red Wings in the first round. The Oilers continued rolling right into the Stanley Cup Finals!

That club set an example for the Edmonton teams that followed. As Messier and his teammates had shown after Gretzky departed, games are not played on paper—they are played on the ice. And the team that plays together and stays together for 60 minutes can accomplish remarkable things.

LEFT: This photo of Mark Messier graced the walls of countless Edmonton fans.   **ABOVE**: Ales Hemsky handles the puck.

HOME ICE

The Oilers have played in the same arena since 1974. The building was constructed for the team and has gone by several different names. During the 2003–04 season, the name changed to Rexall Place, after the company that owned the Oilers. The team's dressing room has a display with **replicas** of five Stanley Cups. There is also an empty space to remind the players that Edmonton fans expect them to win another.

Tickets to Oilers games can be hard to come by, because the arena is one of the smallest in the NHL. Fans had been hoping for a new downtown arena for many years. They finally got their wish, and a new arena was coming for the 2016–17 season.

BY THE NUMBERS

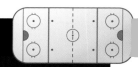

- The Oilers' arena has 16,839 seats for hockey.

- The arena was the first in the NHL to have a scoreboard that hangs above center ice.

- As of 2013, the Oilers had retired seven numbers: 3 (Al Hamilton), 7 (Paul Coffey), 9 (Glenn Anderson), 11 (Mark Messier), 17 (Jari Kurri), 31 (Grant Fuhr), and 99 (Wayne Gretzky).

Fans watch one of the video screens before an Oilers game.

An "oiler" is a name for someone who works in the oil business. Alberta is known as Canada's "energy *province*"—it produces oil, coal, and natural gas. Just north of Edmonton is a huge deposit of **oil sands**, which accounts for more than a third of the country's oil production.

The Oilers have used the same *logo* since they started play in 1972. The team name is spelled out in a circle, with a drop of oil above the lettering. Edmonton's original colors were red, white, and blue. The team changed the red to orange in the mid-1970s. Beginning in the 1990s,

the Oilers made small changes in the shades of the colors and the stripes on the jersey. The team even wore a different logo on special occasions. Since 2008, however, the Oilers have featured uniforms very similar to their look from the 1980s.

LEFT: Jordan Eberle wears the team's away uniform in a 2012–13 game.
RIGHT: This trading card shows Al Hamilton in the team's early years.

WE WON!

When hockey fans talk about the greatest dynasties in NHL history, the Edmonton teams of the 1980s are always near the top of the list. In the eight seasons from 1982–83 to 1989–90,

the Oilers reached the Stanley Cup Finals six times and lost only once. The first of their five championships came in 1983–84, against the New York Islanders.

The year before, the Islanders had **swept** Edmonton in the Stanley Cup Finals. This time, Oilers coach Glen Sather had his players ready. Grant Fuhr opened the series with a 1–0 shutout on New York's home ice. After the Islanders won Game 2, the series shifted to Edmonton. The Islanders were leading Game 3 by a

goal when Mark Messier faked his way past two defenders and rifled a shot into the net to tie the score. The Oilers exploded for five more goals to win 7–2. They blew out the Islanders in the next two games to win the series.

The Oilers faced the young Philadelphia Flyers in the finals the following year and found themselves trailing after Philadelphia won Game 1. Wayne Gretzky took over from there. He scored the winning goal in the next three games. In Game 5, Edmonton overwhelmed the Flyers 8–3 to take the Stanley Cup. Gretzky, Glenn Anderson, and Jari Kurri were unstoppable throughout the playoffs, as Edmonton lost a total of three games against their four postseason opponents.

LEFT: Mark Messier keeps two hands on the Stanley Cup as the Oilers celebrate in 1984.   **ABOVE**: Glenn Anderson scores a goal against the Philadelphia Flyers.

The Flyers were older and battle-tested when the two teams met again in the 1986–87 Stanley Cup Finals. The Oilers won the first two games on their home ice and split the next two on the road. Edmonton fans were ready to celebrate when the series returned to their building for Game 5. But Philadelphia won 4–3, and then tied the series two days later. The Oilers played like champions in Game 7. They drilled 43 shots at goalie Ron Hextall and silenced the Philadelphia attack. Edmonton skated to a 3–1 victory and its third Stanley Cup. Messier, Kurri, and Anderson combined for 41 goals in 21 playoffs games.

Gretzky's fourth and final championship as an Oiler came in 1987–88. Edmonton lost just two games heading into its championship showdown with the Boston Bruins. The Oilers continued their **domination** as they swept the series. Gretzky was indeed The Great One, with 43 points in the postseason. What most fans remember about the Stanley Cup Finals, however, was Game 4 in Boston. A power failure in the second period ended the game tied at 3–3. The statistics from the game counted, but the game itself did not. So the Oilers won in a sweep … in five games!

After his team's victory, Gretzky gathered the Edmonton players for a photo with the Stanley Cup. This became an NHL tradition in the years that followed.

Two seasons later, the Oilers captured their fifth Stanley Cup. They faced the Bruins again. Game 1 was a thriller. It went into triple-**overtime** and became the longest game ever played in the finals. Petr Klima won it for Edmonton. The story of the series was goalie Bill Ranford, who filled in for an injured Fuhr. Ranford allowed only eight goals in five games and won the Conn Smythe Trophy. When the final horn sounded, the Oilers rushed onto the ice to celebrate. Seven of those players had suited up for all five Stanley Cups: Anderson, Fuhr, Messier, Kurri, Randy Gregg, Charlie Huddy, and Kevin Lowe.

LEFT: The Oilers gather around Wayne Gretzky for a memorable Stanley Cup photo in 1988.   **ABOVE**: Bill Ranford was a great replacement for Grant Fuhr during the 1988 playoffs.

GO-TO GUYS

To be a true star in the NHL, you need more than a great slapshot. You have to be a "go-to guy"—someone teammates trust to make the winning play when the seconds are ticking away in a big game. Oilers fans have had a lot to cheer about over the years, including these great stars.

THE PIONEERS

WAYNE GRETZKY   Center

- BORN: 1/26/1961   • PLAYED FOR TEAM: 1978–79 TO 1987–88

Wayne Gretzky was the perfect player for the brand of hockey that became popular in the 1980s. He was a quick and graceful skater, a wonderful passer, and an accurate shooter. Gretzky used these skills to produce four 200-point seasons with the Oilers and lead them to four championships.

KEVIN LOWE   Defenseman

- BORN: 4/15/1959   • PLAYED FOR TEAM: 1979–80 TO 1991–92 & 1996–97 TO 1997–98

Kevin Lowe was Edmonton's first draft pick after the Oilers joined the NHL. He helped them win five Stanley Cups. He also played in the **All-Star Game** seven times. Lowe did not miss a playoff game in 1988, despite a broken wrist and broken ribs.

MARK MESSIER   Center

- BORN: 1/18/1961   • PLAYED FOR TEAM: 1979–80 TO 1990–91

Mark Messier began his career as a left wing. During the 1984 playoffs, coach Glen Sather switched him to center, and Messier blossomed into a superstar. He won the Conn Smythe Trophy that spring and six seasons later won the Hart Trophy as the NHL's MVP.

JARI KURRI   Right Wing

- BORN: 5/18/1960   • PLAYED FOR TEAM: 1980–81 TO 1989–90

Jari Kurri teamed with Wayne Gretzky to form one of the game's greatest goal-scoring duos. Kurri led the NHL in goals in 1985–86 and scored the goal that won the Stanley Cup in 1987. In 2001, he became the first player from Finland to be voted into the Hall of Fame.

PAUL COFFEY   Defenseman

- BORN: 6/1/1961   • PLAYED FOR TEAM: 1980–81 TO 1986–87

Paul Coffey was one of the fastest-skating defensemen in history. He won the Norris Trophy that season as the league's best **blue-liner**. Coffey set a record for defensemen with 48 goals the following season and won his second Norris Trophy.

GRANT FUHR   Goalie

- BORN: 9/28/1962   • PLAYED FOR TEAM: 1981–82 TO 1990–91

Grant Fuhr had all the skills a championship goalie needs—quickness, strength, *anticipation*, and courage. He teamed with Andy Moog and Bill Ranford to give the Oilers great goaltending for 10 seasons.

Esa Tikkanen
OILERS
'90-'91 TEAM SCORING LEADER

ESA TIKKANEN   Left Wing

- BORN: 1/25/1965
- PLAYED FOR TEAM: 1984–85 TO 1992–93

Esa Tikkanen played on the same **line** as Wayne Gretzky and Jari Kurri. His outstanding defense allowed his linemates to take chances and attack the net. Tikkanen also distracted opponents with his "Tikki Talk"—an endless stream of chatter, often in Finnish.

DOUG WEIGHT   Center

- BORN: 1/21/1971
- PLAYED FOR TEAM: 1992–93 TO 2000–01

When the Oilers traded Tikkanen for Doug Weight, they got a young player who knew how to make his teammates better. Weight's excellent skating and passing helped Edmonton make it back to the playoffs after falling short of the postseason four years in a row.

ALES HEMSKY   Right Wing

- BORN: 8/13/1983   • FIRST YEAR WITH TEAM: 2002–03

Ales Hemsky was known more for his passing than his shooting when he came into the NHL at the age of 19. However, he won a place in the hearts of Edmonton fans in the 2006 playoffs for his goal-scoring. Hemsky netted the series-winning goal against the Detroit Red Wings that season.

RYAN SMYTH — Left Wing

- BORN 2/21/1976
- PLAYED FOR TEAM: 1994–95 TO 2006–07 & 2011–12 TO PRESENT

Ryan Smyth used his big body and quick reflexes to become a 30-goal scorer for the Oilers. He specialized in deflecting shots to change their direction. Smyth also had a nose for rebounds, often whacking loose pucks into the net.

SHAWN HORCOFF — Center

- BORN: 9/17/1978
- PLAYED FOR TEAM: 2000–01 TO 2012–13

Shawn Horcoff was a key player in Edmonton's 2006 run to the Stanley Cup Finals. In 2010, he was named team captain. Horcoff ranked among the fastest skaters in team history.

JORDAN EBERLE — Right Wing

- BORN: 5/15/1990
- FIRST SEASON WITH TEAM: 2010–11

Jordan Eberle was the team's top draft pick in 2008. He played in the All-Star Game and became a team leader for the Oilers in his early 20s. His first goal as an Oiler was voted the Goal of the Year for the 2010–11 season.

LEFT: As this trading card shows, Esa Tikkanen knew how to score, too.
ABOVE: Fans were happy when Ryan Smyth returned to the Oilers in 2011.

When Glen Sather joined the Oilers for the 1976–77 season, Edmonton fans didn't think much about the move. Sather was at the end of a playing career that saw him score just 80 goals during nearly 10 years in the NHL. Near the end of his first year with the Oilers, he became the team's **player-coach**. After that, Sather hung up his skates and took over the coaching duties full-time. Over the next few years, he would build one of the greatest teams in NHL history.

The first of Sather's many smart decisions was to encourage team owner Peter Pocklington to get Wayne Gretzky. Everyone knew Gretzky had great skill, but many scouts thought he was too short and frail to stand up to the punishment of **professional** hockey. Sather told Pocklington, "Whatever you have to do, get him." Gretzky actually lived with Sather's family when he arrived in Edmonton.

After the Oilers joined the NHL, Sather took on the added responsibility of running the team's business. He and head scout Barry Fraser worked together to draft and trade for players to surround Gretzky, including Mark Messier, Paul Coffey, Jari Kurri,

Glen Sather (far left) and John Muckler (right) kneel on either side of Wayne Gretzky after Edmonton's 1988 championship.

Glenn Anderson, and Grant Fuhr. Sather coached the Oilers through the 1988–89 season, and again in 1993–94. During his 14 seasons behind the bench, Edmonton went to the playoffs 13 times and won four championships. Even when the Oilers did not have strong teams, Sather was good at trading for players who could succeed in his system.

One of Sather's most trusted advisers was John Muckler. He served as Sather's assistant on the Stanley Cup championships in 1984 and 1985. When Edmonton won the Stanley Cup in 1987 and 1988, Muckler actually shared head coaching duties with Sather. In 1989, Sather stepped aside and made Muckler the full-time coach. Muckler promised the Oilers that they could still be champions without Gretzky, and he was right—he led the team to its fifth championship the following spring.

MAY 31, 1987

When the final buzzer sounded on the Oilers' 1987 Stanley Cup victory, their fans finally felt that everything was right in the world again. One year earlier, Edmonton's season had ended in shocking fashion. In Game 7 of a playoff series against the Calgary Flames, **rookie** Steve Smith accidentally shot the puck into his own net with the score tied 2–2. Smith carried the guilt of this mistake with him throughout the 1986–87 season, and his teammates knew it.

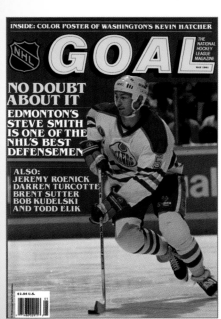

The Oilers made it back to the Stanley Cup Finals that spring, but they struggled throughout their series against the Philadelphia Flyers. Every time it looked as if Edmonton had control of a game, the Flyers fought back. In Game 7, Oilers fans groaned when Philadelphia scored the first goal—it was the first time in the series they had done so.

This time it was the Oilers that fought back. Mark Messier started the comeback with a goal in the first period. Jari Kurri made the score 2–1 on a **wrist shot** in the second period. And Glenn Anderson finished off the Flyers in the third period. His sizzling shot ended the scoring in a 3–1 victory.

As Wayne Gretzky lifted the Stanley Cup, the Edmonton captain pushed through the crowd and handed it to Smith. The young defenseman was floored. His face lit up as he led the Oilers on their victory lap around the rink, holding the cup high above his head. The fans let out a deafening roar. All was forgotten. All was forgiven.

LEFT: Steve Smith was a great player who didn't want to be remembered for one huge mistake.   **ABOVE**: Wayne Gretzky raises the Stanley Cup after Edmonton's victory.

LEGEND HAS IT

WHICH OILER PERFORMED THE MOST PAINFUL GOAL CELEBRATION?

LEGEND HAS IT that Georges Laraque did. A 245-pound forward who played eight seasons for Edmonton, Laraque would fling himself at the protective glass— arms spread wide and face unprotected—after scoring. He once admitted that the move "hurt like crazy" but added that he scored so infrequently that this was the best way he knew how to release all of his excitement and energy. After he retired, Laraque went into politics. He became the Deputy Leader of Canada's ***Green Party***.

ABOVE: Georges Laraque begins his unique goal celebration.

WHO GAVE WAYNE GRETZKY THE IDEA TO WEAR NUMBER 99?

LEGEND HAS IT that Phil Esposito did. Early in Gretzky's career when he was playing for the Sault Ste. Marie Greyhounds, he wanted number 9. But Brian Gualazzi already had it. Gretzky tried a couple of other numbers but was unhappy with them. When his coach pointed out that Phil Esposito had switched from 7 to 77 after joining the New York Rangers, Gretzky agreed to try number 99. He scored two goals his first night and decided to keep the number—and years later went on to break Esposito's record for goals in a season!

WHICH EDMONTON GOALIE TRAVELED BACK IN TIME?

LEGEND HAS IT that Bill Ranford did. After retiring from the Oilers in 2000, Ranford was asked to play for the 1980 U.S. Olympic hockey team. The producers of the film *Miracle* needed someone to play Jim Craig, the goalie who helped America win the gold medal that year. Ranford studied Craig's style and did a perfect imitation of him for the movie.

The 1981–82 season was a special one for Wayne Gretzky. No player in NHL history had ever scored 50 goals in fewer than 50 games. After 37 games that year, Gretzky already had 41 goals. On December 27, the Oilers played the Los Angeles Kings. Gretzky was unstoppable, pumping in four goals in 10–4 victory. That night he passed 100 points to set a record. The fastest anyone had reached 100 points was in 51 games. Phil Esposito did this in 1970–71 when he set the NHL record for goals in a season, with 76.

Three nights later, Gretzky skated onto Edmonton's home ice to a standing ovation. The Oilers were facing a tough team, the Philadelphia Flyers. They were determined to shut Gretzky down. Several times during the game, Philadelphia goalie Pete Peeters stopped him from **point-blank** range.

Gretzky kept attacking the net. He knocked in a rebound off the boards for his first goal. He beat Peeters with a slapshot for his second. Gretzky scored on a breakaway for his third, and then made a great move and shot for his fourth. He now had 49. In the closing minutes, the crowd rose to its feet every time Gretzky

Wayne Gretzky celebrates another record-breaking goal in 1981–82.
This one was his 77th, which set a new NHL mark.

touched the puck. They groaned when he passed up good scoring chances to pass to an open teammate. Late in the game, the Flyers pulled their goalie to gain a man advantage. With five seconds left, Gretzky got the puck from Glenn Anderson, skated a few strides, and fired a shot the length of the ice into Philadelphia's open net for goal number 50.

Gretzky's 50 goals in 39 games set a new standard for scoring. He finished the year with 92 goals to shatter Esposito's record. The Great One's nine goals in two games also set an NHL mark. The fact he did it against a great defense and under such amazing pressure made the night all the more special.

When a team wins five championships, and then doesn't win another for 20-plus years, you might expect to see a lot of empty seats at its games. This is hardly the case in Edmonton. Win or lose, Oilers fans love the team. The NHL will probably never see a collection of talent like the one that played for Edmonton in the 1980s, but fans still expect the team to put good players on the ice. And they expect the Oilers to live up to the examples of Wayne Gretzky, Mark Messier, and the other Hall of Famers.

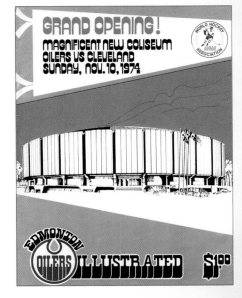

While many NHL teams feel the need to entertain crowds with cheerleaders and mascots, the Oilers know better. To their fans, these ideas are mostly a distraction. The team did try a cheerleading squad once and it was very unpopular. Besides, the fans put on a great show themselves. Blue body paint and orange wigs are a common sight at Oilers games.

LEFT: Showing up to a game in team colors is part of the fun in Edmonton.
RIGHT: This program celebrated the opening of the Oilers' arena.

TIMELINE

The hockey season is played from October through June. That means each season takes place at the end of one year and the beginning of the next. In this timeline, the accomplishments of the Oilers are shown by season.

1978–79
The Oilers finish with the best record in the WHA.

1983–84
The team wins its first Stanley Cup.

1972–73
The team plays its first season as the Alberta Oilers.

1981–82
Wayne Gretzky sets an NHL record with 92 goals.

1984–85
Paul Coffey wins his first Norris Trophy.

This pennant was sold during the team's first season.

Grant Fuhr falls to the ice to make a save in the 1986 All-Star Game.

1985–86
Nine Oilers play in the NHL All-Star Game.

2005–06
The Oilers reach the Stanley Cup Finals for the seventh time.

2006–07
The team retires Mark Messier's number 11.

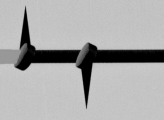

1987-88
The Oilers win their fourth Stanley Cup.

1989–90
The team wins its fifth Stanley Cup.

2011–12
Jordan Eberle is selected to play in the All-Star Game.

Esa Tikkanen and Mike Krushelnyski raise the Stanley Cup together in 1988.

FUN FACTS

KEEPING THE GLOVES ON

Dave Semenko was a big, strong forward who played 10 seasons with the Oilers. During the 1980s, his primary job was to protect his high-scoring teammates from being bullied on the ice by opponents. His reputation as a "fighter" earned him a lot of **notoriety**. He even got a three-round exhibition boxing match with Muhammad Ali.

COFFEY BREAK

Paul Coffey was called the greatest "offensive defenseman" of his time because of his ability to shoot and pass like a forward. In 1985–86, Coffey set a record by notching a goal or assist in 28 games in a row. He scored 55 points during that remarkable streak.

TWO OF A KIND

During the 1970s, many older NHL stars joined the WHA to play one final season or two before retiring. The Oilers had two Hall of Famers in uniform during this time, Jacques Plante and Norm Ullman.

FIRST & LAST

Ron Anderson of the Oilers scored the first goal in WHA history. Edmonton's Dave Semenko scored the last.

LIGHTING THE LAMP

In 1985, in the finals of the Campbell **Conference**, Jari Kurri put on history's greatest goal-scoring show. He had two **hat tricks** in the series, plus a four-goal game. Kurri finished with a total of 12 goals to set a playoff record. His linemate, Wayne Gretzky, also set a record, with 14 assists.

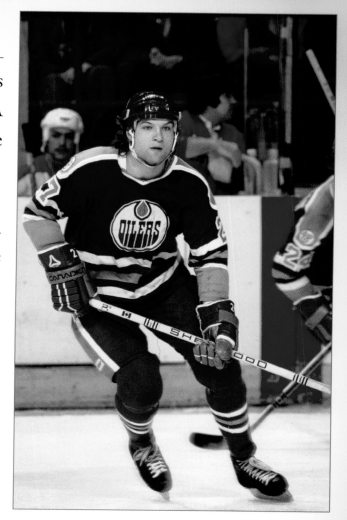

BUCKING THE SYSTEM

Bill Flett was known as "Cowboy" because he owned a ranch in Alberta and also competed in rodeos. When Flett played for the Oilers, he was one of the only professional hockey players with a full beard—and one of the last to play without a helmet.

ABOVE: Dave Semenko was known more for his intimidating play than his goal-scoring.

TALKING HOCKEY

"They all grew up together. They were willing to learn and willing to do whatever it took to win."

▶ **GLEN SATHER,** *on the team chemistry of the Oilers in the 1980s*

"A good hockey player skates to where the puck is. A great hockey player skates where the puck is *going* to be."

▶ **WAYNE GRETZKY,** *on the importance of always thinking a step ahead*

"Everything's in front of you. You see it all. You see everything develop, you see where to go."

▶ **PAUL COFFEY,** *on what he liked about being a defenseman*

"I enjoy taking **faceoffs** … it's a great one-on-one battle in the game and I like doing it."

▶ *SHAWN HORCOFF, on being Edmonton's go-to guy on faceoffs*

"The guys have to like each other, they have to treat each other as family. That's the biggest thing we had in Edmonton."

▶ *GRANT FUHR, on what carried the Oilers through the playoffs*

"When I sat in that dressing room with all those great players—when I looked around the room and we were in a big game—the one guy I thought would score the big goal was Anderson."

▶ *KEVIN LOWE, on teammate Glenn Anderson*

"My jersey hanging from the ceiling is going to be a symbol of the hard work of the people I played with."

▶ *MARK MESSIER, on having his number retired by the Oilers*

LEFT: Glen Sather
ABOVE: Shawn Horcoff

GREAT DEBATES

People who root for the Oilers love to compare their favorite moments, teams, and players. Some debates have been going on for years! How would you settle these classic hockey arguments?

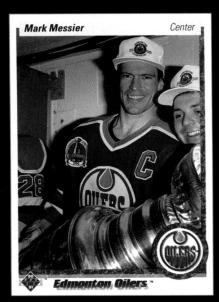

Mark Messier — Center

Edmonton Oilers

MARK MESSIER WAS THE OILERS' GREATEST LEADER . . .

. . . because he took over as captain when Wayne Gretzky was traded and led the team to the Stanley Cup. No one thought the Oilers could win a championship after The Great One left for Los Angeles. Messier (**LEFT**) proved them wrong. If there was any doubt what kind of leader he was, look what happened after he joined the New York Rangers. Messier led them to their first Stanley Cup in more than 50 years!

THEY DIDN'T CALL GRETZKY THE GREAT ONE FOR NOTHING . . .

. . . because he was a great leader as well as a great player. The Oilers had the talent to win the Stanley Cup in the early 1980s, but they always fell short. When Lee Fogolin stepped aside to let Gretzky become captain at age 22 in 1983–84, the Oilers took the final step and grabbed their first Stanley Cup.

PAUL COFFEY WAS EDMONTON'S ALL-TIME BEST DEFENSEMAN ...

... because he is the only Oiler to win the Norris Trophy. Coffey earned the award twice with the team and smashed several NHL records. He was a good defender and a great team player. Coffey holds the record for goals (48) by a defenseman in a season, as well as the most points (8) by a defenseman in one game.

FOR PURE DEFENSE, KEVIN LOWE WAS THE BEST OF ALL-TIME ...

... because when Coffey was working his give-and-go with Wayne Gretzky, Lowe (RIGHT) was the team's last line of defense. He didn't get many goals or assists, but he did his job—**checking** and blocking shots—as well as his high-scoring teammates did their jobs. Lowe was a key man on five championship teams for Edmonton. He was also an All-Star six times. Would the Oilers have won those Stanley Cups without Lowe? Maybe not!

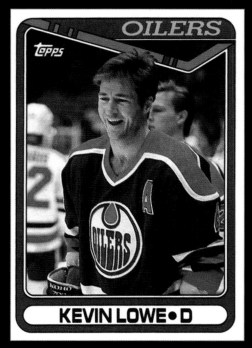

KEVIN LOWE • D

FOR THE RECORD

The great Oilers teams and players have left their marks on the record books. These are the "best of the best" …

OILERS AWARD WINNERS

Dave Dryden

Grant Fuhr

ART ROSS TROPHY
TOP SCORER

Wayne Gretzky	1980–81
Wayne Gretzky	1981–82
Wayne Gretzky	1982–83
Wayne Gretzky	1983–84
Wayne Gretzky	1984–85
Wayne Gretzky	1985–86
Wayne Gretzky	1986–87

HART MEMORIAL TROPHY
MOST VALUABLE PLAYER

Wayne Gretzky	1979–80
Wayne Gretzky	1980–81
Wayne Gretzky	1981–82
Wayne Gretzky	1982–83
Wayne Gretzky	1983–84
Wayne Gretzky	1984–85
Wayne Gretzky	1985–86
Wayne Gretzky	1986–87
Mark Messier	1989–90

VEZINA TROPHY
TOP GOALTENDER

Grant Fuhr	1987–88

ALL-STAR GAME MVP

Wayne Gretzky	1982–83
Grant Fuhr	1985–86

JAMES NORRIS MEMORIAL TROPHY
TOP DEFENSEMAN

Paul Coffey	1984–85
Paul Coffey	1985–86

CONN SMYTHE TROPHY
MVP DURING PLAYOFFS

Mark Messier	1983–84
Wayne Gretzky	1984–85
Wayne Gretzky	1987–88
Bill Ranford	1989–90

JACK ADAMS AWARD
COACH OF THE YEAR

Glen Sather	1985–86

WHA MVP*

Dave Dryden	1978–79

WHA ROOKIE OF THE YEAR

Wayne Gretzky	1978–79**

* Known as the Gary Davidson Award & Gordie Howe Trophy.

** Also played for the Indianapolis Racers.

OILERS ACHIEVEMENTS

ACHIEVEMENT	YEAR
AVCO Cup Finalists	1978–79
Campbell Conference Champions	1982–83
Campbell Conference Champions	1983–84
Stanley Cup Champions	1983–84
Campbell Conference Champions	1984–85
Stanley Cup Champions	1984–85
Campbell Conference Champions	1986–87
Stanley Cup Champions	1986–87
Campbell Conference Champions	1987–88
Stanley Cup Champions	1987–88
Campbell Conference Champions	1989–90
Stanley Cup Champions	1989–90
Western Conference Champions	2005–06

JARI KURRI • RW

ABOVE: Jari Kurri starred for all five of Edmonton's championship teams.
LEFT: Ales Hemsky scores the goal that sent the Oilers to the 2006 Stanley Cup Finals.

PINPOINTS

The history of a hockey team is made up of many smaller stories. These stories take place all over the map—not just in the city a team calls "home." Match the pushpins on these maps to the **TEAM FACTS**, and you will begin to see the story of the Oilers unfold!

TEAM FACTS

1. Edmonton, Alberta—*The Oilers have played here since 1972.*
2. Brantford, Ontario—*Wayne Gretzky was born here.*
3. Lachute, Quebec—*Kevin Lowe was born here.*
4. Vancouver, British Columbia—*Glenn Anderson was born here.*
5. Brandon, Manitoba—*Bill Ranford was born here.*
6. Banff, Alberta—*Ryan Smyth was born here.*
7. Trail, British Columbia—*Shawn Horcoff was born here.*
8. Warren, Michigan—*Doug Weight was born here.*
9. Buffalo, New York—*Todd Marchant was born here.*
10. Pardubice, Czech Republic—*Ales Hemsky was born here.*
11. Helsinki, Finland—*Jari Kurri was born here.*
12. Glasgow, Scotland—*Steve Smith was born here.*

Wayne Gretzky

GLOSSARY

HOCKEY WORDS

VOCABULARY WORDS

ALL-STAR GAME—The annual game that features the best players from the NHL.

ANTICIPATION—Expecting something to happen before it does.

ASSISTS—Passes that lead to a goal.

BLUE-LINER—Another term for a defenseman.

BLUEPRINT—A detailed plan used to build something.

CHECKING—Using the body to knock into an opponent.

CONFERENCE—A large group of teams. There are two conferences in the NHL, and each season each conference sends a team to the Stanley Cup Finals.

DOMINATION—Complete control through the use of power.

DRAFT CHOICES—Players selected in the annual meeting during which NHL teams pick the top high school, college, and international stars.

FACEOFFS—Battles for the puck that occur after play stops. Two players "face off" against each other as the referee drops the puck between them.

GREEN PARTY—A Canadian political party formed in 1983.

HALL OF FAME—The museum in Toronto, Canada, where hockey's best players are honored. A player voted into the Hall of Fame is sometimes called a "Hall of Famer."

HAT TRICKS—Three-goal games by an individual player.

LINE—The trio made up by a left wing, center, and right wing.

LOGO—A symbol or design that represents a company or team.

MOST VALUABLE PLAYER (MVP)—The award given each year to the league's best player; also given to the best player in the playoffs and All-Star Game.

NATIONAL HOCKEY LEAGUE (NHL)—The professional league that has been operating since 1917.

NOTORIETY—Fame, usually as the result of something negative.

OBLIGED—Did something as a favor.

OIL SANDS—Sandy areas that contain natural resources such as oil.

OVERTIME—An extra period played when a game is tied after three periods. In the NHL playoffs, teams continue to play overtime periods until a goal is scored.

PLAYER-COACH—A player who also coaches a team.

PLAYOFFS—The games played after the season to determine the league champion.

POINT-BLANK—So close it's almost impossible to miss.

POSTSEASON—Another term for playoffs.

PROFESSIONAL—A player or team that plays a sport for money.

PROVINCE—A region of Canada, somewhat similar to a state.

REPLICAS—Exact copies.

ROOKIE—A player in his first season.

STANLEY CUP—The trophy presented to the NHL champion. The first Stanley Cup was awarded in 1893.

STANLEY CUP FINALS—The final playoff series that determines the winner of the Stanley Cup.

SWEPT—Won a series without losing a game.

UPSET—Beat a team that was favored to win.

WORLD HOCKEY ASSOCIATION (WHA)—The professional league that operated from 1972 to 1979.

WRIST SHOT—A shot taken by "flicking" the puck with a quick turn of the wrists.

LINE CHANGE

TEAM SPIRIT introduces a great way to stay up to date with your team! Visit our **LINE CHANGE** link and get connected to the latest and greatest updates. **LINE CHANGE** serves as a young reader's ticket to an exclusive web page—with more stories, fun facts, team records, and photos of the Oilers. Content is updated during and after each season. The **LINE CHANGE** feature also enables readers to send comments and letters to the author! Log onto:

www.norwoodhousepress.com/library.aspx

and click on the tab: **TEAM SPIRIT** to access **LINE CHANGE**.

Read all the books in the series to learn more about professional sports. For a complete listing of the baseball, basketball, football, and hockey teams in the **TEAM SPIRIT** series, visit our website at:

www.norwoodhousepress.com/library.aspx

ON THE ROAD

EDMONTON OILERS
11230 110 Street
Edmonton, Alberta, Canada T5G 3H7
(780) 414-4000
http://oilers.nhl.com

HOCKEY HALL OF FAME
Brookfield Place
30 Yonge Street
Toronto, Ontario, Canada M5E 1X8
(416) 360-7765
http://www.hhof.com

ON THE BOOKSHELF

To learn more about the sport of hockey, look for these books at your library or bookstore:

- Cameron, Steve. *Hockey Hall of Fame Treasures*. Richmond Hill, Ontario, Canada: Firefly Books, 2011.

- Keltie, Thomas. *Inside Hockey! The legends, facts, and feats that made the game*. Toronto, Ontario, Canada: Maple Tree Press, 2008.

- Romanuk, Paul. *Scholastic Canada Book of Hockey Lists*. Markham, Ontario, Canada: Scholastic Canada, 2007.

INDEX

PAGE NUMBERS IN **BOLD** REFER TO ILLUSTRATIONS.

Ali, Muhammad 36
Anderson, Glenn 9, 13, 17, **17**,
        18, 19, 25, 27, 31, 39, 45
Anderson, Ron 37
Arnott, Jason 10
Carson, Jimmy 10
Coffey, Paul 9, **9**, 13, 21,
        24, 34, 36, 38, 41, 42
Craig, Jim 29
Dryden, Dave 6, 42, **42**
Eberle, Jordan **14**, 23, 35
Esposito, Phil 29, 30, 31
Flett, Bill 6, 37
Fogolin, Lee 40
Fraser, Barry 24
Fuhr, Grant 9, 10, 13, 16, 19,
        21, 25, **35**, 39, 42, **42**
Gagner, Sam 4
Gelinas, Martin 10
Gregg, Randy 19
Gretzky, Wayne 7, **8**, 9, 10, 11,
        13, 17, 18, 19, 20,
        21, 22, 24, 25, **25**, 27,
        27, 29, 30, 31, **31**, 33, 34,
        37, 38, 40, 41, 42, 45, **45**
Gualazzi, Brian 29
Hall, Taylor 4
Hamilton, Al 6, 13, **15**
Harrison, Jim 6
Hemsky, Ales 11, **11**, 22, **43**, 45
Hextall, Ron 18
Horcoff, Shawn 11, 23, 39, **39**, 45
Huddy, Charlie 19
Joseph, Curtis 10
Klima, Petr 10, 19
Krushelnyski, Mike **35**

Kurri, Jari 9, 13, 17, 18, 19,
        21, 22, 24, 27, 37, **43**, 45
Langevin, Dave 7
Laraque, Georges 28, **28**
Long, Barry 6
Lowe, Kevin 9, 19, 20,
        22, 39, 41, **41**, 45
Marchant, Todd 10, 45
McDonald, Blair 6
Messier, Mark 9, 10, **10**,
        11, 13, **16**, 17,
        18, 19, 21, 24, 27,
        33, 35, 39, 40, **40**, 42
Moog, Andy 21
Muckler, John 25, **25**
Peca, Michael 10
Peeters, Pete 30
Plante, Jacques 6, **6**, 36
Pocklington, Peter 24
Pronger, Chris 10
Ranford, Bill 10, 19, **19**,
        21, 29, 42, 45
Roloson, Dwayne 11
Samsonov, Sergei 11
Sather, Glen 7, 16, 21, 24,
        25, **25**, 38, **38**, 42
Semenko Dave 36, 37, **37**
Shmyr, Paul 7
Smith, Steve 26, **26**, 27, 45
Smyth, Ryan 10, 11, 23, **23**, 45
Stoll, Jarret 11
Tikkanen, Esa 22, **22**, **35**
Torres, Raffi 11
Ullman, Norm 36
Weight, Doug 10, 22, 45
Yakupov, Nail **4**

THE TEAM

MARK STEWART has written over 200 books for kids—and more than a dozen books on hockey, including a history of the Stanley Cup and an authorized biography of goalie Martin Brodeur. He grew up in New York City during the 1960s rooting for the Rangers, but has gotten to know a couple of New Jersey Devils, so he roots for a shootout when these teams play each other. Mark comes from a family of writers. His grandfather was Sunday Editor of *The New York Times*, and his mother was Articles Editor of *Ladies' Home Journal* and *McCall's*. Mark has profiled hundreds of athletes over the past 25 years. He has also written several books about his native New York and New Jersey, his home today. Mark is a graduate of Duke University, with a degree in history. He lives and works in a home overlooking Sandy Hook, New Jersey. You can contact Mark through the Norwood House Press website.

DENIS GIBBONS is a writer and editor with *The Hockey News* and a former newsletter editor of the Toronto-based Society for International Hockey Research (SIHR). He was a contributing writer to the publication *Kings of the Ice: A History of World Hockey* and has worked as chief hockey researcher at five Winter Olympics for the ABC, CBS, and NBC television networks. Denis also has worked as a researcher for the FOX Sports Network during the Stanley Cup playoffs. He resides in Burlington, Ontario, Canada with his wife Chris.